EMDR WITH KIDS

Flip Chart

A Play-Based Tool for Trauma Processing, Nervous System Regulation, and the Transformation of Adaptive Behaviors

Jackie Flynn, EdS, LMHC-S, RPT-S™

EMDR with Kids Flip Chart

Published by
PESI Publishing, Inc.
3839 White Ave
Eau Claire, WI 54703

Cover and interior design by Amy Rubenzer
Editing by Jenessa Jackson, PhD

ISBN 9781683737728 (print)
ISBN 9781683737742 (ePDF)

Printed in the United States of America.

PESI Publishing
pesipublishing.com

About the Author

Jackie Flynn, EdS, LMHC-S, RPT-S™, is a licensed psychotherapist, registered play therapist supervisor, child trauma therapist, and a certified Safe and Sound Protocol provider. She hosts Play Therapy Community®, where clinicians gather together from around the world to share resources and inspire each other. As a cohost of the Neuroscience of Play Therapy Summit and Playful EMDR Summit, as well as the founder of EMDR and Play Therapy Integration Support, she supports countless international clinicians in learning about the power of play through training and consultation.

About This Flip Chart

Dear EMDR-trained child therapist,

I'm pleased to introduce you to a valuable resource that can enhance your understanding of EMDR therapy with children and teenagers.

Working with young clients who have experienced trauma demands specialized skills and a deep commitment to their well-being. Typically, though, basic EMDR training only focuses on how EMDR works with adults, leaving child therapists feeling stuck and in search of kid-friendly resources that meet the unique needs of children's and adolescents' developing nervous systems.

That is why I decided to create the *EMDR with Kids Flip Chart*. It has been thoughtfully designed to provide you with a practical starting point for integrating play therapy techniques into EMDR while staying true to the eight-phase framework. Given the great influence of Drs. Stephen Porges and Daniel Siegel on me as a clinician, the importance of safety, connection, and coregulation are interwoven through the chart at every opportunity.

Designed for use during client sessions and parent consultations, each page of the chart contains a colorful client-facing side with play- and art-based activities, as well as a grayscale therapist-facing side with supplementary information, directions, and sample scripts. Throughout the chart, you'll also have a friendly companion in Detective BrainBody, a curious cartoon character symbolizing the autonomic nervous system. Detective BrainBody adds a touch of playfulness and care to your sessions.

It's important to note that if you are not trained in EMDR therapy, this flip chart is not suitable for you. Foundational training in EMDR therapy is required to use this resource in a safe and effective way.

As you go through this chart, I hope you add your own creative touch to it. Let it be a starting point to ignite your clinical creativity, allowing you to tailor your approach to each unique young client you work with. Together, let's embark on this healing journey, rooted in the integration of play and the relational safety you offer!

Take care,

Jackie

Jackie Flynn, EdS, LMHC-S, RPT-S™

Table of Contents

Introducing EMDR Therapy

Client View

Sample Script

When something happens that is just too much for the brain and body to handle, you can sometimes feel, act, sleep, and even think differently. You can even feel stuck!

EMDR can help your body work through these situations so you can feel better. To do so, we're going to use this playful chart together during your EMDR therapy. Throughout the chart, Detective BrainBody will be with you and me every step of the way so that you're never alone in this process.

One of the most common questions EMDR-trained child therapists have is "How do I explain EMDR to my child clients?" Simplicity is key. Overexplaining can lead to resistance and confusion.

Detective BrainBody, a cartoon character representing the autonomic nervous system, is available to help you explain EMDR to children. As a detective, he is curious about what is happening in the body and mind, which supports mindful attention to the state of the nervous system. He playfully moves through the eight phases of this flip chart with you and your client to maintain familiarity and predictability.

Before explaining EMDR to your clients, consider practicing the explanation a few times with a friend. When you feel competent and comfortable explaining it to a friend, you can then use the sample script above to help you formulate an explanation in your own words.

Introducing EMDR Therapy

Phase 1:
History Taking and Case Conceptualization

Client View

Remember

- **Adapt to the child:** Tailor your approach to meet the child's unique needs, and avoid pressuring them to participate.
- **Collaborate with caregivers:** Involve caregivers when it's safe and beneficial.
- **Consider phase 2:** If the child has complex trauma, consider postponing information gathering and moving to phase 2 to establish safety and tolerance.
- **Create a supportive atmosphere:** Maintain a playful and supportive atmosphere to build trust.
- **Use continuous information gathering:** Continuously gather information in each session to guide treatment effectively.

Description

Phase 1 is the initial step in EMDR therapy with children. During this phase, you will work to understand the child's unique needs, strengths, and challenges to prepare for effective trauma processing.

Goals

- **Assess readiness:** Evaluate the child's emotional stability and readiness for EMDR therapy.
- **Identify potential targets:** Discover distressing memories or circumstances that will be the focus of therapy.
- **Assess resources:** Identify the child's internal and external resources, including strengths and support systems.
- **Explore obstacles:** Examine any secondary gains or barriers hindering progress.

Gathering Information

HELLO

my name is

All About Me

Client View

Sample Script

In this activity, I get to learn about you. There are lots of different sentences here that you can finish up in whatever way feels right for you. I'm so curious to learn more about you, so please share as much or as little as you're comfortable with. This is a safe and welcoming space for you to tell your story.

You can start by choosing which sentence to respond to first, either through drawing or writing—or you can just tell me with your words.

Remember, your story is important, and I feel honored to hear it.

Objective

This activity serves as a valuable, structured tool to gather essential information from your client. It enables you to gain insights into their personal history, experiences, strengths, and challenges, ultimately helping you conceptualize the case with an understanding of how the child views their reality.

Description

In this activity, clients will have a chance to share their personal narratives by filling in the blanks to several open-ended sentence prompts. The prompts cover a broad range of topics to provide an overview of the client's life.

All About Me

I love . . .

And I don't like . . .

Something good that happened was . . .

_____ helps me when things get hard.

I wish . . .

And I don't wish . . .

Random facts about me are . . .

Something hard that happened was . . .

My Batteries

Client View

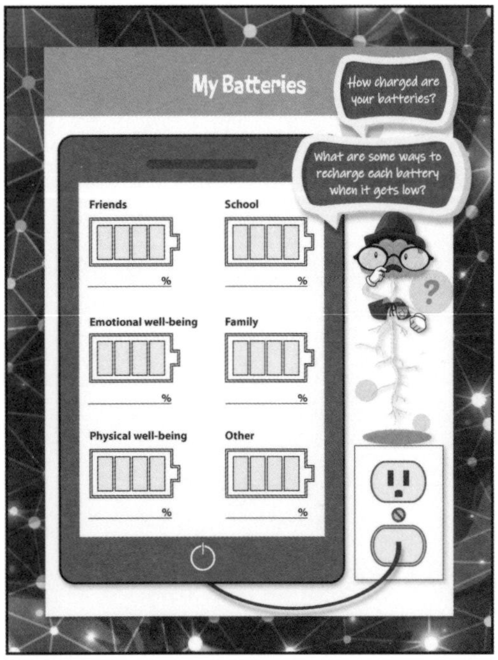

Sample Script

Sometimes, I think of wellness as being similar to the battery in my tablet. I can see how charged my tablet is by looking at the battery symbol on the screen. When it's fully charged, I know I can accomplish what needs to be done.

However, when the battery is running low, I'm not as able to get things done. At that point, I have to connect my tablet into an outlet to recharge it.

Just like the battery levels in electronic devices can go up and down, your energy levels in different parts of your life can change. I'm curious about how charged your "batteries" are right now in each part of your life.

How charged would you like them to be? And how do you think you can recharge them?

Objective

This activity* can reveal a child's potential targets (things that "deplete" their batteries), resources (things that help them "recharge" their batteries), and secondary gains (benefits they get from not "recharging" their batteries).

Description

Many children understand that batteries are used to supply power to electronic equipment. This activity uses the metaphor of an electronic tablet with a variety of batteries to assist you in gathering information about various areas of the child's life, including their friends, school, family, emotional well-being, and physical well-being.

---

* *My Batteries* was inspired by Dr. Matthew Munyon's *iWell* activity with children and is adapted here with permission: M. Munyon, personal communication, February 27, 2020.

My Batteries

How charged are your batteries?

What are some ways to recharge each battery when it gets low?

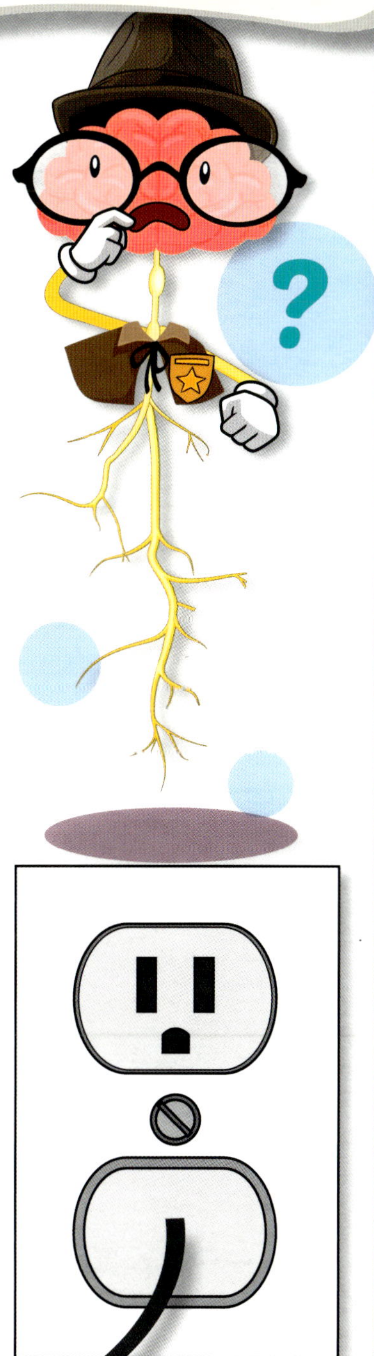

Friends

_______ %

School

_______ %

Emotional well-being

_______ %

Family

_______ %

Physical well-being

_______ %

Other

_______ %

My Resource Bank

Client View

Sample Script

Imagine this piggy bank can hold all your valuable resources.

Resources can be anything you find helpful when things feel hard. This includes activities you already do, items you already have, people you trust, and even your beloved pets.

What are some of your resources? You can write or draw them on the golden coins.

Objective

This activity increases a client's awareness of their current resources, which enhances safety in later phases (phases 3 through 7) of EMDR therapy. It provides a playful representation of children's inner and external resources.

Description

It's crucial for clients to have more "good" stuff (e.g., helpful practices, strengths, pets, supportive people) than "tough" stuff (e.g., pain) before you move beyond the preparation phase. This activity strengthens a client's awareness of what resources they find helpful. In many cases, helping your client identify the resources they already have can boost their motivation to continue with EMDR therapy, as these resources often create positive feelings.

My Resource Bank

Listening to music helps me when I feel upset. What or who is helpful to you when things are hard?

Phase 2:
Preparation

Description

Phase 2 is a critical step in EMDR therapy. It's about establishing trust, creating safety, teaching emotion regulation skills, and introducing therapy in a way that children can understand.

Client View

Goals

- **Explain EMDR therapy:** Use kid-friendly language to describe what EMDR is and what will happen.
- **Build trust:** Create a safe and playful environment with your client to develop a strong therapeutic bond.
- **Learn to balance the nervous system:** Help the child regulate through playful movement, breathwork, and more.
- **Enhance resources:** Identify and strengthen the child's inner and outer strengths.
- **Introduce bilateral stimulation mechanisms:** Familiarize the child with eye movement, sounds, or movement used in EMDR therapy.

Remember

- **Invest time and energy in preparation:** Prioritize thorough preparation in EMDR therapy with traumatized children. It's like the saying "an ounce of prevention is worth a pound of cure." Go beyond creating a safe space and container; focus on building and strengthening as many resources as possible.
- **Do ongoing preparation in every session:** Phase 2 preparation is not a one-time task. It should be an integral part of every session. Maintain a strong therapeutic relationship through non-directive play, continuously help the child develop inner and external resources, and keep an eye on affect management to ensure safety throughout the trauma work.
- **Relational safety is key:** Never underestimate the importance of relational safety in EMDR therapy. Building a strong therapeutic relationship is essential, and the reciprocity of play can be a powerful change agent. Prioritize the child's emotional safety and well-being throughout the entire process.

Getting Ready

Felt Sense of Emotions

Client View

Sample Script

Today, we're going to explore different feelings and how they can show up in your body. This includes feelings like happiness, sadness, anger, and fear.

Each of these feelings has a special job. For example, fear helps keep you safe, sadness lets you know when something is missing from your life, and anger motivates you to take action when necessary.

Now, I want you to look at these pictures of feelings. Can you notice where you feel each one in your body? Maybe when you're happy, your tummy feels warm and light. Or when you're angry, your face might get hot.

All these feelings are okay, as they help us in different ways. In our sessions, we can learn cool things to help you feel even better when you want to. What do you think?

Objective

This activity serves as a resource for clients to use outside of therapy. It enhances emotional literacy regarding primary emotions and fosters an understanding of the felt sense of emotions, which promotes whole-body integration by connecting top-down and bottom-up processes.

Description

This tool features a visual representation of primary emotions, helping children identify and understand these emotions on a bodily level. This supports the integration of emotional awareness and physical sensations. By recognizing that emotions serve specific purposes, you can work together with your client to help them explore and better manage these feelings, giving them more control over how they respond to a variety of emotions.

Felt Sense of Emotions

Pause Button

Client View

Sample Script

Let's talk about something special you have in your EMDR toolbox: the pause button. You can imagine that it's like a pause button on a real remote control. Just like you can use a real remote to press pause on your favorite show, you can use this button if you ever feel like you need a break during our sessions. All you need to do is let me know by saying, "Pause, please!" or some other way that feels right for you.

We'll stop right there, and you can take all the time you need, just like when you pause a game. We'll only start again when you're ready and comfortable. Remember, you're in charge, and I'm here to support you every step of the way!

Objective

The pause button is a concept designed to empower children with a sense of agency during EMDR, particularly in phase 4 (desensitization). It offers them the ability to pause the process at any point, which promotes safety and control. It's essential to honor their request to pause, ensuring they feel respected and supported in their therapeutic journey.

Description

This visual aid features a pause button on an imaginary remote control, much like the one a child might use for their favorite video game. This button is provided to give them a sense of agency, control, and safety during sessions. If, at any point, they feel the need for a break or simply wish to pause, all they have to do is say, "Pause, please!" You will then immediately stop and wait for the child to indicate when they are ready to continue. This tool ensures the child feels comfortable and in control, enhancing their overall sense of safety.

Pause Button

My Strength Shields

Client View

Sample Script

Take a look at these strength shields! Each shield has its own special word representing a strength that some people believe they possess. Let's explore them together.

I'd like you to select any words that you feel describe you. Once you've made your choices, let me know.

[After they select a word]

Now, thinking about the word ________ [chosen word from the following page] *and* ________ [the child's name], *can you share a memory or thought that comes to mind?*

Objective

This activity* is designed to nurture a child's inner resources during therapy, especially as part of the preparation for phase 2 of EMDR therapy.

Description

My Strength Shields presents a curated list of strength words that the child, or their caregiver, can choose from that resonate with the child's character. Once the preferred words are chosen, facilitate a discussion about events or situations that illustrate the child's embodiment of these strengths.

Before the activity, it's helpful to have a conversation with the caregiver emphasizing the positive focus of this exercise. Encourage the caregiver to avoid mentioning any perceived weaknesses or lack of listed strengths in the child. If the selection process becomes challenging or no words are chosen, you should smoothly pivot to another activity, ensuring the atmosphere remains supportive and nonjudgmental. This approach is pivotal in establishing trust and ensuring relational safety.

---

* *My Strength Shields* was inspired by Tammi Van Hollander's *Greatness Sticks* activity: Mellenthin, C. (2018). *Play therapy: Engaging & powerful techniques for treatment of childhood disorders* (pp. 107–109). PESI Publishing & Media. It is also available on YouTube: https://www.youtube.com/watch?v=-tkZxCUvvUM

My Strength Shields

Peaceful Place Doodle

Client View

Sample Script

On this page, you'll see some drawings of different calm places that others have thought of. They might give you some ideas to create your own peaceful place.

Now, can you think of your own special place where you feel calm and safe? Do you have a picture of it in your mind? Awesome! Could you draw or describe that place for me on this page?

While you're drawing, consider the details: What things can you see there? Are there any sounds you might hear? How about things you can touch or feel? Maybe there are smells or even tastes that come to mind? Together, we'll make your peaceful place come alive.

Objective

This activity is designed to foster a child's ability to construct a serene mental space, serving as a key component of phase 2 in EMDR therapy. It bolsters a child's capacity to regulate their emotions by engaging with sensory-rich imagery.

Description

This following page presents a range of illustrations that depict tranquil environments. These examples are intended to provide the child with a foundational understanding of what a peaceful place is and to set the stage for them to envision and detail their own peaceful setting. Follow the child's lead as you delve into the sensory specifics of their peaceful place—sights, sounds, tactile sensations, scents, and potential tastes—to further animate this envisioned sanctuary.

Peaceful Place Doodle

Tough Stuff Container

Client View

Sample Script

Can you think of a special box or container where you can place things that bother you or make you sad? It should have a lid so you can close it up.

Think about what it looks like and tell me when you have it in mind. Got it? Let's see how it works by trying it out.

Objective

The container activity is designed to help kids handle residual disturbance, both during and outside of sessions. Some kids find this activity very helpful while others do not, so it's essential to view the container as a *potential* resource for your client and respect their feedback, especially if they express that it's not preferable or effective for them.

Description

In this activity, your client will create a real or imagined container where they can "put" any difficult feelings or memories. They can pick from one of the examples on the page or create one of their own. You can even make a physical container together in session if you wish. In this special container, they can store drawings, notes, or just thoughts that might be bothering them. Make sure to adapt the kind of container (and what goes into it) to fit what the child likes and needs. After making or thinking of their container, you can test it out with something a bit upsetting but not too severe.

Tough Stuff Container

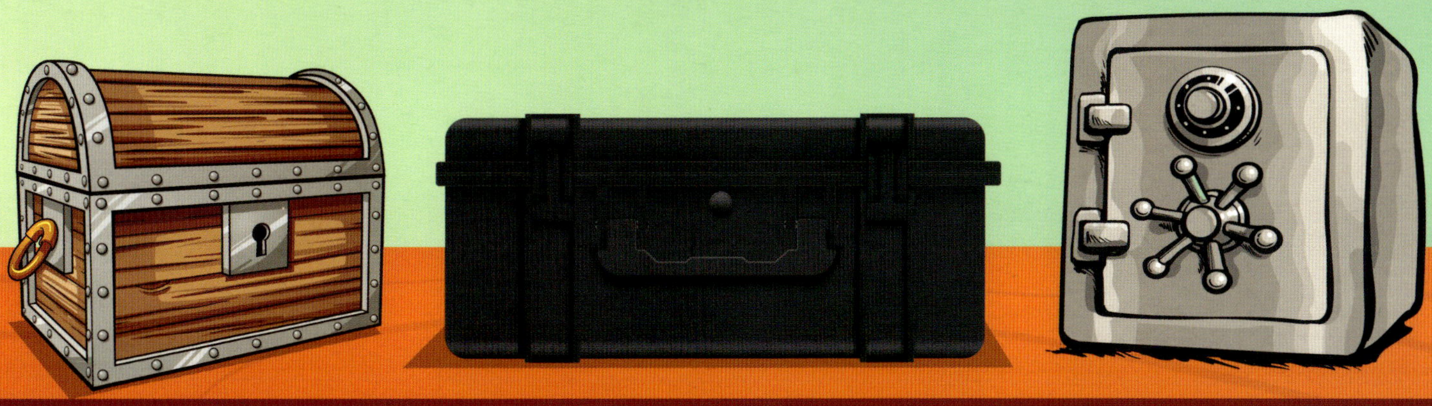

Games of Reciprocity

Client View

Sample Script

Have you ever played Tic-Tac-Toe or I Spy? Tic-Tac-Toe is game where we take turns putting X's and O's on a grid and try to get three in a row. And I Spy is a game where one of us describes something we see without naming it, and the other person tries to guess what that is.

If you're not sure about these games, we can learn together! You can also come up with your own game if you want. Which game do you want to try first?

Objective

This activity aims to foster relational safety through the reciprocity of play. Using a "my turn, your turn" approach in games, children can immerse themselves in an atmosphere where they recognize they're not alone. This playful engagement promotes the simultaneous experience of safety and distress, strengthening resilience and bonding.

Description

On this page, there are straightforward instructions for classic games like Tic-Tac-Toe and I Spy. In Tic-Tac-Toe, two players take turns placing their symbol (either an X or an O) on a grid, aiming to get three of their symbols in a row. I Spy is a guessing game where one player describes something they see, and the other guesses what it is. These games are designed to promote choice and autonomy, allowing the child to decide things like who goes first, whether they'd like to be X's or O's, and when the game ends.

Games of Reciprocity

Tic-Tac-Toe

I Spy

Window of Tolerance

Client View

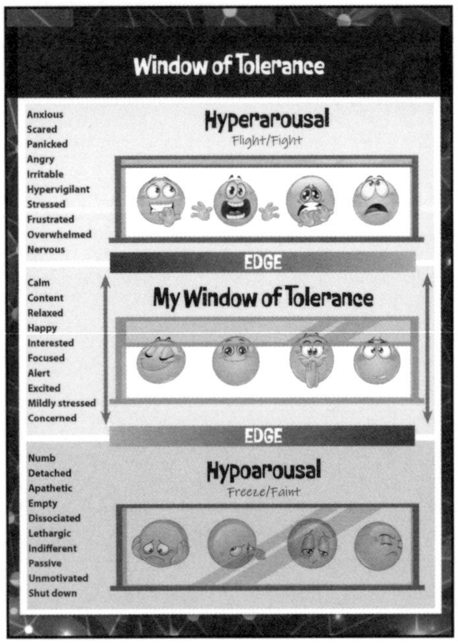

Sample Script

Let's imagine that your feelings are like a window. When your window is wide open, you can feel really frustrated or scared. Here is where you might have the urge to fight or run away when things get hard.

But when your window is almost closed, you can feel really sad and disconnected. Here you might freeze or feel like you may faint when things get hard.

Sometimes, during our EMDR playtime, you might feel like you're almost on the edge. It can feel a little strange, but don't worry, you'll still be safe and we'll be together. This is just a part of how we help you feel better.

Our goal is to find that "just right" spot where your window is not too open and not too closed. This is known as your window of tolerance. In this place, you feel calm, relaxed, and able to focus.

Look at these words to help you understand your feelings better.

As we work together, we'll both pay attention to how you are feeling so you can stay in your window of tolerance or at the edges of your window. That way, we can help you feel better.

Objective

This visual aid will help you explain the concept of emotional arousal to children and parents. It's particularly valuable during phase 2 (preparation) and phase 4 (desensitization), as it can guide clinical decisions regarding emotion regulation.

Description

This tool uses a metaphor of a literal window to visually represent the different emotional states that clients can feel, especially under stress. The emotion words on the graphic align with Dr. Dan Siegel's concept of the window of tolerance, ranging from *hyperarousal* (a wide-open window) to *hypoarousal* (a nearly closed window). You can share this tool with clients as a visual reference to promote collaborative exploration of the client's emotional zone, which can sometimes include the "edge."

Window of Tolerance

Hyperarousal

Flight/Fight

Anxious
Scared
Panicked
Angry
Irritable
Hypervigilant
Stressed
Frustrated
Overwhelmed
Nervous

EDGE

My Window of Tolerance

Calm
Content
Relaxed
Happy
Interested
Focused
Alert
Excited
Mildly stressed
Concerned

EDGE

Hypoarousal

Freeze/Faint

Numb
Detached
Apathetic
Empty
Dissociated
Lethargic
Indifferent
Passive
Unmotivated
Shut down

Phase 3:
Assessment

Description

Phase 3 is a critical step in EMDR therapy that involves identifying and understanding the child's target memory, sensations, emotions, and beliefs to prepare for processing.

Client View

Goals

- **Playfully light up the neural network:** Engage the child in a playful manner to prepare for assessment.
- **Identify the target:** Determine the specific memory or issue to address in therapy.
- **Identify the worst part:** Clarify the most distressing aspect of the memory or issue.
- **Describe the image (or other sensory representation):** Explain any images, sounds, or sensations related to the target.
- **Identify the negative cognition:** Pinpoint the negative belief or thought connected to the target.
- **Establish a positive cognition:** Create a positive belief to replace the negative one.
- **Recognize emotions:** Acknowledge the emotions tied to the target memory or issue.
- **Locate the felt sense of emotions:** Determine where in the child's body they feel these emotions.
- **Rate the subjective unit of distress (SUD):** Assess the child's distress level on a scale of 0–10.
- **Evaluate the validity of cognition (VOC):** Gauge how valid the negative belief feels to the child at present.

Remember

- **Take a non-directive approach:** Share responses gathered from your attuned experience instead of asking the child multiple questions.
- **Make sure to play:** Play allows for the child to experience safety and distress at the same time, which increases their capacity for processing.

Setting Up Our Target

How Much? (SUD Rating Scale)

Client View

Sample Script

This tool lets us see how you are feeling as we work to address the memory or issue that's bothering you. If something feels just a little bothersome, it might be a low number, like 0 or 1. However, if something feels very, very troubling, it could be a bigger number, like 9 or 10. Always remember, it's okay to share your feelings in your own special way.

As we work together on this special memory or issue, the number might not always change right away. That's alright! Everybody works at their own pace, and I'm here to give you all the time you need without any rush or expectation.

Objective

This kid-friendly SUD scale is designed to gauge a child's level of distress linked to a specific target or memory. Understanding this distress guides your next steps clinically, especially in phase 4. It's crucial for the SUD to be at a 0—or at a level that feels naturally acceptable based on the intensity of the target—before moving on to phase 5. If the distress level is still significant, then it wouldn't make sense to install the positive cognition or perform a body scan, as it can increase somatic intensity. In such cases, it's better to proceed to phase 7 (closure) to regulate the client effectively before leaving the session if the distress level is still elevated, meaning it's not at an ecologically valid level or 0.

Description

This scale uses both imagery and numbers to assist kids in expressing the intensity of their disturbance. While numbers offer a way for kids to convey their distress levels, it's important to appreciate each child's uniqueness. Some children may choose to express the intensity in a different way that feels most authentic to them, be it through words, drawings, or another avenue.

How Much?

How True? (VOC Rating Scale)

Client View

Sample Script

This tool lets us see how much your thoughts and beliefs feel real to you. Do you see the pictures of the mushrooms growing and the numbers from 1 to 7? These mushrooms are growing based on how true something feels!

If a thought feels just a tiny bit true, it's like a small mushroom, closer to 1. And if it feels very, very true, it's like a big mushroom, near 7.

Let's try it! How true does [cognition] *feel for you?*

But guess what? You can show or tell me about how true your thoughts feel in any fun way you want! You can use words, stretch your arms wide, or pick a toy. Whatever you like best!

Objective

This kid-friendly VOC scale is designed to help you gauge a child's perception of the validity of a cognition, or how true a thought or belief feels to them. By assessing the belief's perceived truthfulness, you can better navigate the therapeutic process, especially during phase 3 (assessment) and phase 5 (installation).

Description

This scale helps kids visualize and express how real or right a thought or idea feels to them. It does so via the imagery of the growth stages of a mushroom, paired with a scale from 1 to 7. Even though the scale offers a structured way to share how valid a cognition might seem, it's vital to understand that children can express their perceptions in any way that makes sense to them. This might be through words, but it can also be through actions like moving their arms, using toys, or employing any other method they find meaningful.

How True?

I am strong.
I am lovable.
I belong.
I am smart.
I look good.

I did the best I could.
I can make mistakes.
I do my best.
I learned from it.

I matter.
I am good enough.
I deserve good things.
I am a good person.
I am fine just the way I am.

I am safe now.
I can choose whom to trust.
I can trust myself.
I can show and feel
my emotions.

I have choices.
I can handle it.
I am free.
I can succeed.
I have control.

How True?

Step by Step: Procedural Steps Pathway

Client View

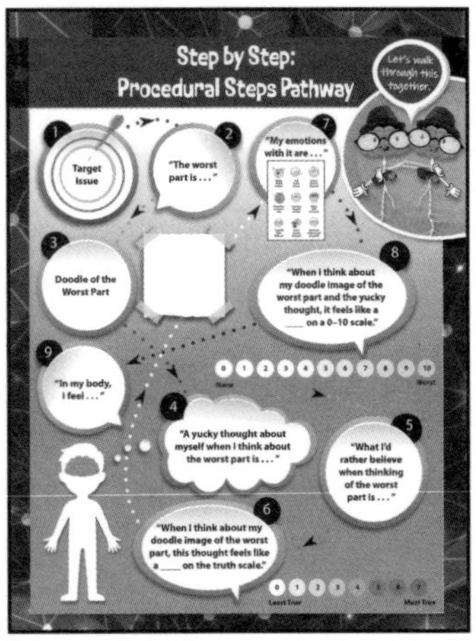

Objective

This step-by-step page is designed to assist you in activating neural networks before phases 4 through 7. This activity should only be undertaken when it can be immediately followed by reprocessing in phases 4 through 7, as it can be distressing. Please remember that this resource is intended solely for EMDR-trained clinicians.*

Sample Script

Let's take a look at this special step-by-step page. It's a helpful tool that we'll use on our journey together to understand and work through your feelings and thoughts in a special way. You can think of it like a map!

1. *Let's figure out together what to target.*
2. *Can you tell me what the worst part is?*
3. *Now, doodle out an image that represents the worst part.*
4. *I wonder if the tough thought that goes with that doodle is* ___________. [Suggest a negative cognition using your clinical judgment, then wait to have it confirmed or corrected by the client. Work together until you identify the most fitting one. Remember, there can be only one negative cognition.]
5. *I wonder if you'd rather believe* ___________. [Suggest a positive cognition. It's okay to think of more than one positive cognition.]
6. *On a scale of 1 to 7, how true do those positive words feel, where 1 is "not true at all" and 7 is "the most true"?*
7. *When you look at your doodle and think about* ___________ [restate the negative cognition], *what emotions do you feel now?*
8. *How disturbing does this feel in your body right now? Rate it from 0 to 10, where 0 is "not disturbing at all" and 10 is "the most disturbing."*
9. *Where do you feel that in your body?*

Description

This page offers a helpful guide to navigate the procedural steps of phase 3 in a bilateral fashion. These steps involve exploring various aspects of a distressing memory, such as the worst part, negative thoughts, positive thoughts, and more, while engaging both the right and left sides of the brain.

---

* Shapiro, F. (2018). *Eye movement desensitization and reprocessing: Basic principles, protocols, and procedures* (3rd ed.). Guilford Press.

Step by Step: Procedural Steps Pathway

1 Target Issue

2 "The worst part is . . ."

3 Doodle of the Worst Part

4 "A yucky thought about myself when I think about the worst part is . . ."

5 "What I'd rather believe when thinking of the worst part is . . ."

6 "When I think about my doodle image of the worst part, this thought feels like a ____ on the truth scale."

0 1 2 3 4 5 6 7

Least True — Most True

7 "My emotions with it are . . ."

8 "When I think about my doodle image of the worst part and the yucky thought, it feels like a ____ on a 0–10 scale."

0 1 2 3 4 5 6 7 8 9 10

None — Worst

9 "In my body, I feel . . ."

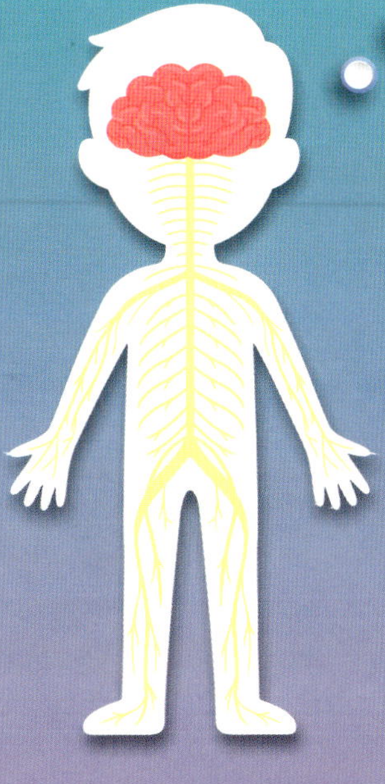

Phase 4:
Desensitization

Description

Phase 4 is a pivotal stage in EMDR therapy that involves processing the target issue by pairing it with adaptive beliefs and using bilateral stimulation.

Client View

Goals

- **Direct the client to pair the image with the negative cognition:** Instruct the child to connect the distressing image with their negative belief.
- **Begin bilateral stimulation (fast):** Initiate eye movement, sounds, or tapping to facilitate processing.
- **Return to the target as appropriate:** Encourage the child to explore the memory while maintaining focus on the image and belief.
- **Notice adaptive shifts:** Observe shifts toward more positive beliefs or reduced distress.
- **Check the SUD:** Assess the child's distress level on a scale of 0–10.
- **If the SUD is 0 or ecologically valid, proceed to phase 5:** If the child's distress is minimal or the belief feels valid, move on to the installation phase.
- **If the SUD is still elevated, proceed to phase 7:** If the child's distress persists, move to the closure phase to stabilize emotions and return to processing later.

Remember

- **Take a non-directive approach:** Use playful bilateral stimulation methods that fit the child's needs and pace. You don't need to ask the client a list of questions; instead, track and comment on their responses while remaining deeply attuned to the client through play.
- **Promote safety:** Ensure the child feels safe and supported during processing.
- **Observe shifts:** Pay attention to any positive changes in the child's beliefs or emotional state.
- **Use flexible progression:** Progress to the next phase based on the child's SUD level and readiness for further processing.

Feeling Better

Butterfly Tap

Client View

Sample Script

Let's explore something cool called the butterfly tap! It's a playful and helpful way to make yourself feel better. Here's how you do it:

Cross your arms, interlock your thumbs, place your hands (palms down) on your chest, and then tap on each side of your body, just like butterfly wings. Give it a try!

Tap, tap, tap. You can use it whenever you need to feel better or when we're working on things together. It's like having your own special way to help you feel better!

Objective

The butterfly tap is a self-administered form of bilateral stimulation, which is a technique used in EMDR therapy to help the brain process and integrate distressing memories and emotions. We aim to introduce this playful and helpful technique to children as one of several options for bilateral stimulation during therapy sessions.

Description

This is a valuable resource that allows you to teach your client how to perform bilateral stimulation on themselves. This technique can aid in both processing and resourcing during EMDR therapy, providing a playful alternative for children to use as part of their therapeutic toolkit.

Butterfly Tap

Bilateral Waves

Client View

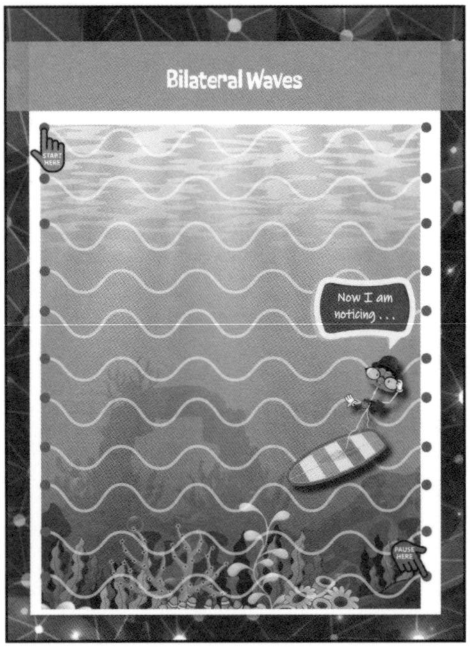

Sample Script

We're going to ride the bilateral waves. Imagine you're underwater in the ocean, and there are soft waves moving from one side to the other. Take your finger and trace these wavy lines from left to right, just like the waves in the sea.

While you do this, notice what's happening with your thoughts and in your body. When I say pause, let me know what thoughts you have and what you feel in your body.

It's like going on an underwater adventure together while we work on helping you feel better!

Objective

This activity is designed to assist children in engaging in bilateral stimulation in a playful manner, promoting dual awareness within the context of an underwater theme during EMDR therapy.

Description

For this activity, the child will visualize a vibrant underwater scene, where gentle waves flow from left to right. Encourage them to use their finger to trace the wavy lines on the page while noticing their thoughts and bodily sensations. This visual exercise can be adapted in length and complexity based on the child's needs.

Bilateral Waves

Animal in Me

Client View

Sample Script

You get to choose which animal you want to be today: a gorilla, a penguin, a cat, a T-Rex, or an elephant.

When you've picked your animal, show me how they would move from left to right. It's like being your favorite animal while we work together to help you feel better.

Which animal do you want to be today?

Objective

This activity is intended to provide children with playful bilateral stimulation options during EMDR therapy. It encourages movement and allows children to embody their favorite animals, fostering engagement and participation.

Description

For this activity, encourage your client to explore left-right motion. They can choose from various animals, each with its unique bilateral movement:

- **Gorilla chest taps:** Mimicking a gorilla, the child can gently tap their chest with both hands, moving from left to right.
- **Penguin waddle:** Channeling their inner penguin, the child can waddle like a penguin, shifting their weight from one foot to the other, creating a rhythmic left-right movement.
- **Cat paw swipe:** Like a cat, they can softly swipe their hands back and forth in front of them, alternating between left and right.
- **T-rex hop:** Imagining themselves as a T-rex, they can perform small hops from one foot to the other, creating a playful left-right rhythm.
- **Elephant trunk swing:** Emulating an elephant's trunk, they can gently swing their arms, moving them from left to right.
- You can also get creative and add more animals or movements to adapt the experience to each child's preferences and therapeutic goals.

Animal in Me

Move from left to right!

Gorilla Chest Pound

Cat Paw

T-Rex Hop

Penguin Waddle

Elephant Trunk Swing

Phase 5: Installation

Description

In phase 5, the primary focus is on transforming the negative thought associated with the target memory into a positive belief. This positive belief is then firmly anchored within reality, enhancing its sense of truth and authenticity by pairing it with a representation of the previously identified "worst part."

Client View

Goals

- **Re-evaluate the positive cognition identified in phase 3:** You want to ensure the positive cognition's continued relevance or find a more suitable replacement if necessary. You can assist the child in identifying the most fitting positive belief. For example: "Does 'I am strong' still fit the helpful thought of what you'd like to believe when you think of your doodled image? It can change if you need."
- **Pair the target image with the positive cognition:** You can also pair the positive cognition with an alternative sensory representation (e.g., sound, smell) of the most distressing part. Then initiate bilateral stimulation. The choice between fast bilateral stimulation (to address any remaining emotional residue) or slow bilateral stimulation (for resourcing) depends on your clinical judgment of the situation.

Remember

- **Connect it to the body:** Installation can be further strengthened through playful embodiment, encouraging the child to use their body to represent the positive belief.
- **Keep it playful:** Maintain a playful and connected atmosphere during the shared experience to ensure the child feels comfortable and engaged.
- **Allow the positive cognition to be unique to the child:** Make sure to use kid-friendly and meaningful language. Flexibility is key, and metaphors can be a powerful tool to enhance generalizability, such as "I am the mountain."

Positive Thoughts

My Positive Thoughts

Client View

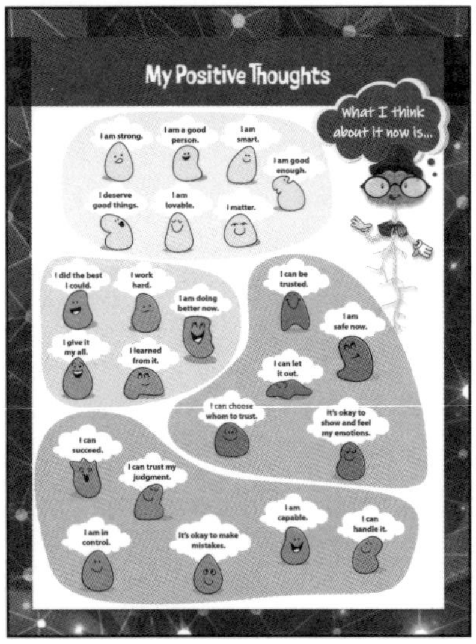

Sample Script

This page has a collection of helpful thoughts that can make you feel better. See these categories? Each one has positive thoughts that can make you feel strong, safe, and happy.

Take a look and pick a thought that feels just right for you. And if you have your own positive thought that's not here, you can use that too! It's all about choosing what helps you the most on our journey together.

Objective

This activity is designed to help children reconnect with and choose positive cognitions during phase 3 (assessment) and phase 5 (installation) in EMDR therapy. It categorizes positive cognitions into four key areas, providing structure while allowing flexibility. Children should also know that they can use positive thoughts not listed on the page.

Description

This is a visually engaging page for children. It includes positive cognitions grouped into four categories:

- **Self:** Positive thoughts about the self, like "I am good" or "I am strong."
- **Responsibility:** Positive thoughts about taking charge and being responsible, like "I did the best I could" or "I learned from it."
- **Safety/vulnerability:** Positive cognitions focused on feeling safe and protected, like "I am safe now" or "I can choose whom to trust."
- **Control/choice:** Positive thoughts emphasizing control and choice, like "I am capable" or "I can handle it."

You will want to help your client explore and select positive cognitions that resonate with them. They should also understand that if they have their own positive thoughts, they can use those as well. In EMDR therapy, clients can select and utilize multiple positive cognitions, which is different from negative cognitions, where typically only one is chosen. Positive cognitions play a pivotal role in EMDR therapy.

My Positive Thoughts

I am strong.
I am a good person.
I am smart.
I am good enough.
I deserve good things.
I am lovable.
I matter.

I did the best I could.
I work hard.
I am doing better now.
I give it my all.
I learned from it.

I can be trusted.
I am safe now.
I can let it out.
I can choose whom to trust.
It's okay to show and feel my emotions.

I can succeed.
I can trust my judgment.
I am capable.
I can handle it.
I am in control.
It's okay to make mistakes.

Phase 6:
Body Scan

Client View

Remember

- **Practice somatic awareness:** Assist the child in noticing their body sensations through playful means, like using a magnifying glass or flashlight. You can also strengthen the positive cognition by asking the child to name a pose that represents it.
- **Use effective bilateral stimulation:** Use bilateral stimulation when needed to ease physical discomfort and ensure the child's comfort.

Description

Phase 6 is an important part of EMDR therapy for children. It's about connecting positive beliefs with memories while paying attention to body sensations to reveal any residual disturbance and work through them if necessary.

Goals

- **Connect memory with positive belief:** Help the child link challenging memories or issues from phases 3 and 4 with their positive beliefs while noticing body sensations.
- **Notice body sensations:** Encourage the child to be aware of any feelings of tightness, tension, or anything unusual in their body.
- **Use fast bilateral stimulation for somatic distress:** If the child experiences physical discomfort, provide rapid bilateral stimulation until the distress lessens, or for as long as it helps. Bilateral stimulation can be natural movements, such as hopping, walking, playing with something with both hands, and so forth.

Body Scan

Felt Sense Doodle

Client View

Sample Script

Do you see this blank body shape? It's like a map for your body sensations.

Hold the special image and the positive thought _________ [fill in the positive thought verbally] *in your mind. Then, scan your body from the bottom of your feet to the top of your head and draw what you feel and where you feel it on the body shape on this page.*

Objective

This is a tool designed to support a child's awareness of and connection to sensations within their body during EMDR therapy. It provides a neutral body shape that allows the child to express their felt sense, aiding in the body scan process. Its purpose is to help the child detect any remaining disturbance or unprocessed material, even if their SUD level has reduced to 0 or an ecologically valid rating. If any disturbance is detected, it guides you to use fast bilateral stimulation to process it through.

Description

The *Felt Sense Doodle* features a blank body shape where the child can express the sensations they feel within their body. To use the tool, direct the child to hold the target image and a positive thought (which you will determine at the time) and then scan their body, starting from the bottom of their feet and moving all the way up to the top of their head. The goal is to notice any tightness, tension, or unusual sensations. This process helps detect any lingering disturbance or unprocessed material, even if their emotional distress has significantly reduced. If such disturbance is identified, bilateral stimulation is employed to facilitate its processing.

Felt Sense Doodle

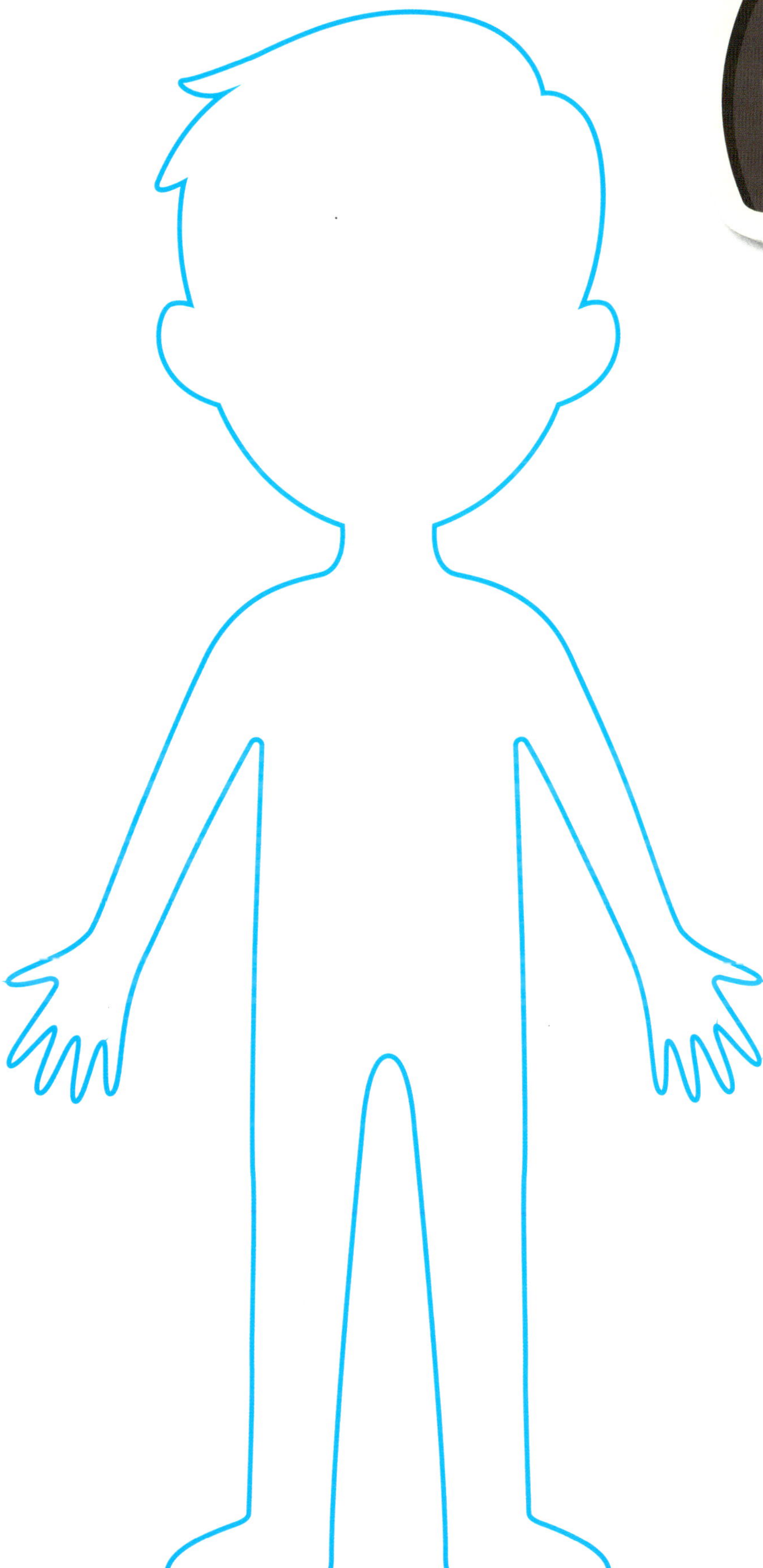

Head, Shoulders, Knees, and Toes Body Scan

Client View

Sample Script

Let's do something playful with a head, shoulders, knees, and toes body scan! Think about the special image and positive thought we talked about earlier.

Now, as we sing "Head, Shoulders, Knees, and Toes," pay attention to how you feel in those parts of your body. It will be a playful game that we play together. Ready?

Objective

This activity is designed to engage children in a playful and whole-brain experience during phase 6 (body scan). It is designed to help them become aware of any residual disturbance, if present, while maintaining their positive cognition from phase 5 (installation).

Description

This interactive activity is designed for you to do together with the child. To begin, direct the child to recall their original image and positive cognition from phase 5 (installation). As the child thinks about this, playfully guide them to notice what they feel in their "head, shoulders, knees, and toes" by saying these body parts in a singsong rhythm to the tune of the well-known song. This playful activity helps make any potentially disturbing material accessible to the child while they maintain their positive thoughts.

Head, Shoulders, Knees, and Toes Body Scan

Flashlight Feelings

Client View

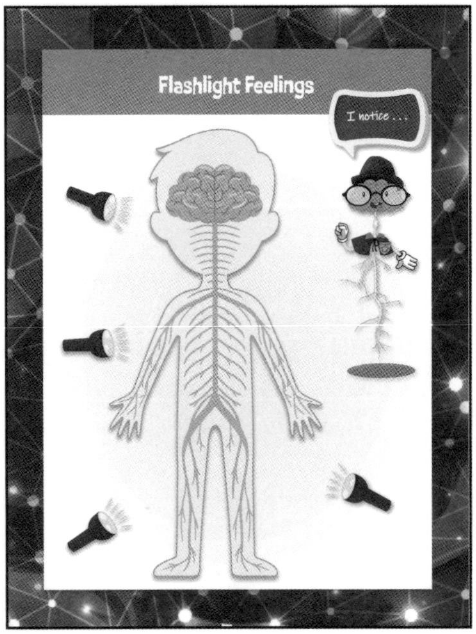

Sample Script

Let's have some fun with Flashlight Feelings! Imagine you have a special flashlight in your mind. This flashlight can find any feelings that might still be hiding inside you.

Hold your special image and positive thought in your mind while we use this flashlight together. If the flashlight shows you any feelings that are still there, just let me know, and we'll use it to help those feelings feel better.

Objective

This is a playful and imaginative activity to help children become aware of any lingering distress associated with the target. If a child reports finding any remaining distress, use bilateral stimulation at a fast pace to process it through while maintaining a playful atmosphere.

Description

This activity works best when you actively join in with the child, as the shared experience enhances the child's sense of safety and trust. To begin, guide the child to bring their target image and positive cognition to mind while picturing a special flashlight. This special flashlight has the remarkable ability to reveal and address any remaining distress related to the target issue or memory.

During this playful activity, if the child reports that the flashlight has discovered any remaining distress, you will want to employ fast bilateral stimulation to help process it through. The focus is on keeping the experience playful throughout.

Flashlight Feelings

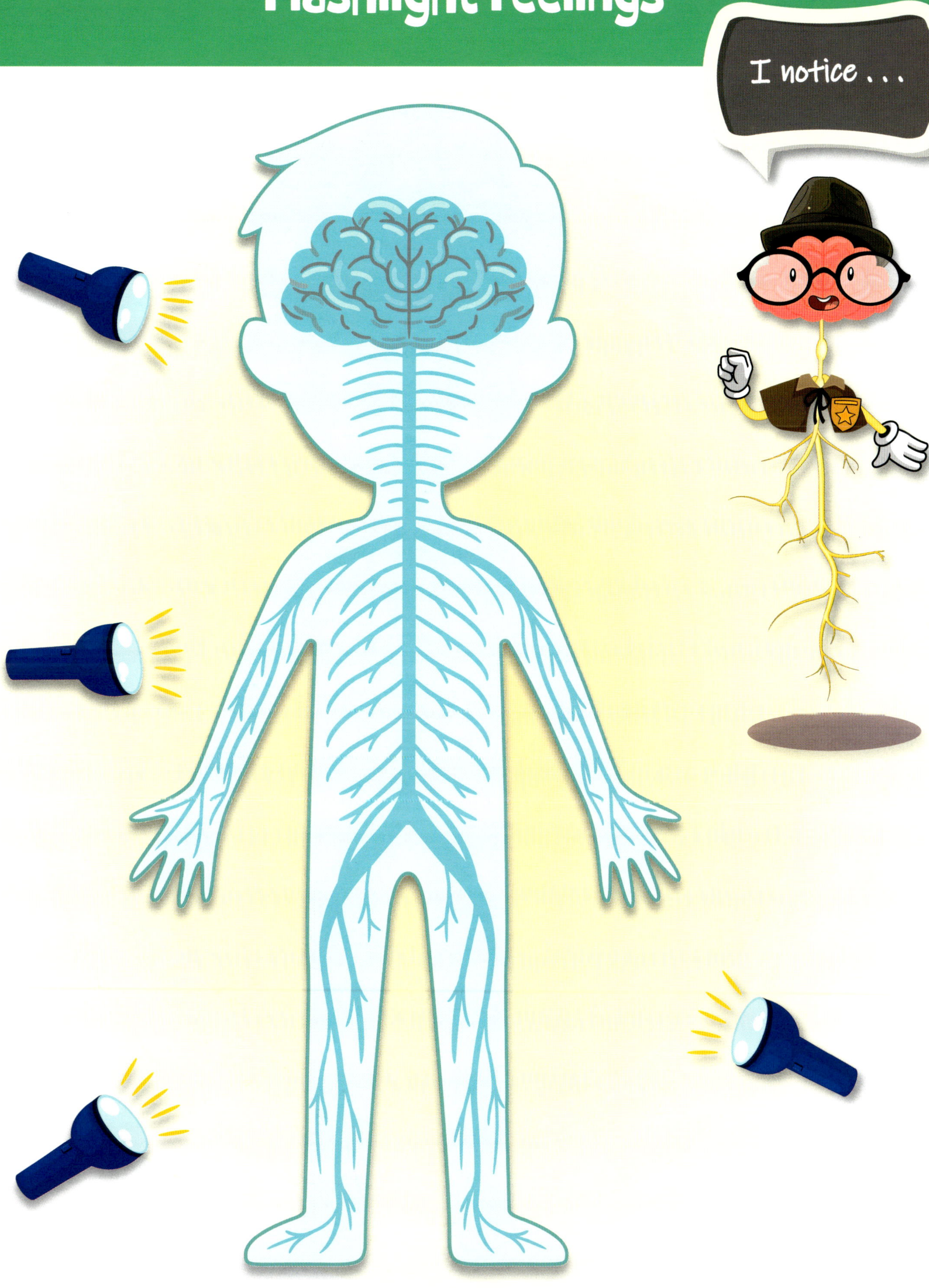

Phase 7:
Closure

Client View

Remember

- **Keep it playful:** Closure should be a connected and active experience, not a checklist of tasks. Incorporate movement, sounds, and sometimes even nature to make it appealing to the child. Make it as fun and playful as appropriate.
- **Don't rush it:** Give the child the time they need to fully engage in the closure process. Rushing may disrupt the sense of safety and connection.
- **Encourage reciprocity:** Foster a sense of cooperation and collaboration between you and the child during play. Allow the child to make choices and take the lead in activities.
- **Create a transition space:** Arrange the play therapy area near the exit and provide fidgets and games of reciprocity to ease the child's transition back to their caregiver, making it a smoother process.

Description

In phase 7 of EMDR therapy, called *closure*, the focus is on helping the client regain emotional stability and return to a regulated nervous system. This allows them to transition back to their daily life without feeling emotionally overwhelmed or dysregulated from the session. Closure is achieved through the therapeutic application of play and occurs right before the end of the session.

Goals

- **Promote nervous system regulation:** Assist the child in regulating their emotions to provide a stable foundation for leaving the session and going back to their daily routine with emotional balance.
- **Return to a state of balance:** Use playful activities to help the child reset after EMDR therapy and achieve a state of emotional equilibrium.

Relaxation Time

5-4-3-2-1 Grounding

Client View

Objective

This activity is designed to help children settle their nervous system during phase 7 (closure) of EMDR therapy. It serves to center and ground the child, allowing them to regain emotional equilibrium.

Sample Script

Let's play 5-4-3-2-1 Grounding together! For this activity, we'll use our senses to help us feel regulated and centered.

To begin, look around and tell me five things you can see. [Pause]

Then listen carefully and tell me four things you can hear. [Pause]

Now tell me three things you can touch around you. [Pause]

Next, tell me two things you can smell, or picture smelling something really wonderful in your mind. [Pause]

Finally, tell me one thing you can taste, or imagine tasting something that you really enjoy. [Pause]

You can also practice this activity outside of our sessions to help you feel better.

Description

For this activity, guide the child to identify:

- Five things they can see
- Four things they can hear
- Three things they can touch
- Two things they can smell
- One thing they can taste

This sensory exploration helps the child reconnect with the present moment and facilitates emotion regulation. If certain sensory experiences, like smell or taste, are not accessible at the moment, encourage the child to use their imagination and picture something pleasant. Above all, make sure to engage in this exercise *with* the child, making it a shared experience that promotes a sense of calm and safety.

5-4-3-2-1 Grounding

5 things I can see . . .

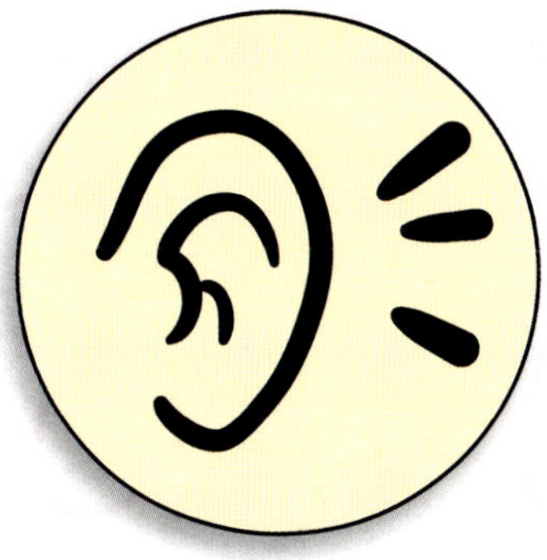

4 things I can hear . . .

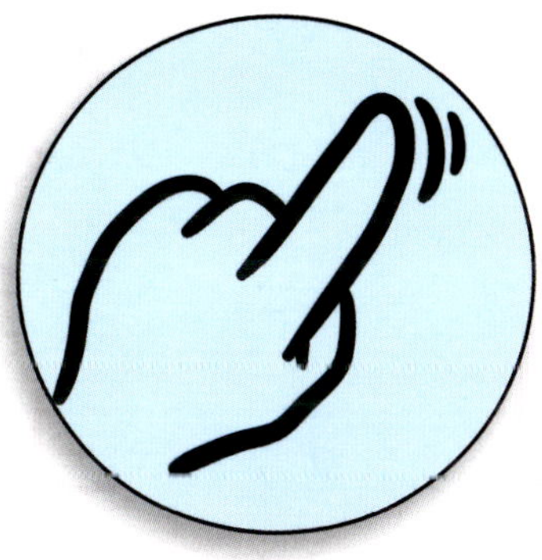

3 things I can touch . . .

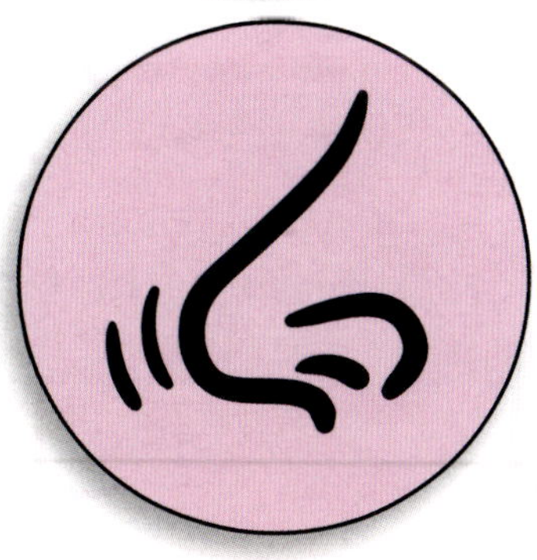

2 things I can smell . . .

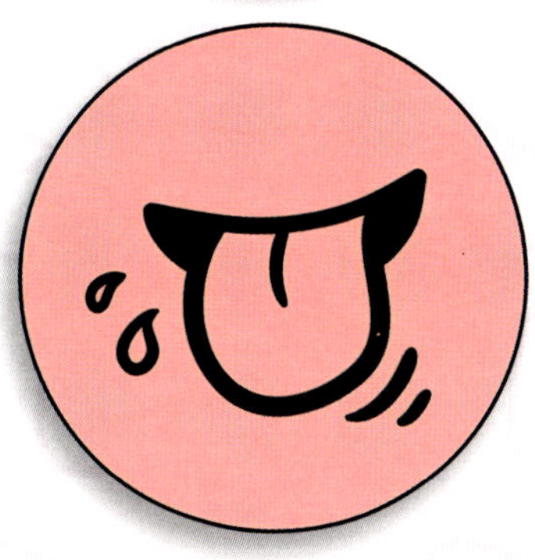

1 thing I can taste . . .

Rainbow Colors

Client View

Sample Script

Let's play a game together! For this game, we'll start by imagining a rainbow in our minds and name the colors together. Ready? Red, orange, yellow, green, blue, indigo, and violet. These colors can help us feel calm and balanced.

Now let's take turns seeing what we can find around us that are colors of the rainbow. Let's start with red!

Oh, I see a red ______. [name a red object you see] *What about you?* [pause]

Let's keep playing with the remaining colors in the rainbow! [continue taking turns naming things around you that are orange, yellow, green, blue, indigo, and violet]

You can also play this with your family at home to have even more fun together.

Objective

This activity serves as a playful and therapeutic turn-taking game that supports the child during phase 7 (closure) of EMDR therapy. It can also be employed during phase 2 (preparation) as well as whenever the child needs grounding, such as during abreactions. It encourages mindfulness and assists in closing out the session, helping the child regain emotional equilibrium before moving on with their day. Parents can also be encouraged to engage in this playful activity as a family.

Description

This activity is a robust way to regulate emotions, offering a playful progression from easy-to-find, common colors to more challenging and less common ones. This gradual shift allows the child to become increasingly grounded and engaged in the therapeutic process, creating a strong foundation for emotion regulation and connection with you.

Rainbow Colors

Heart Labyrinth

Client View

Sample Script

Let's explore the Heart Labyrinth together! Pretend you're helping a little mouse find some yummy cheese by tracing the path with your finger. While you do this, take slow breaths and notice how your body feels.

Objective

This activity is designed to provide support to a child during phase 7 (closure) of EMDR therapy. It offers a playful and mindful option to help them settle their nervous system at the end of a session, fostering a sense of calm and equilibrium.

Description

This activity features a maze-like labyrinth that presents a delightful challenge for a tiny mouse to find its way to the cheese. For the child, this means tracing their finger through the labyrinth's winding paths. It's a playful and engaging exercise that encourages mindfulness and can assist the child in concluding the session on a soothing note.

Heart Labyrinth

Sky Breathing

Client View

Sample Script

Let's go on a sky breathing adventure together. Imagine we're lying down, looking up at the sky.

Then we'll breathe in for four seconds, filling our bodies with calm and peaceful blue skies.

We'll hold our breath for a moment, counting to seven in our heads.

Then we'll breathe out for a count of eight, letting go of any worries or tension, just like gray clouds drifting away.

Together, we'll feel more relaxed and in control.

Objective

This activity is a versatile tool designed to support children during phase 7 (closure) of EMDR therapy. However, it can also be used whenever the child needs to return to a state of regulation, especially after experiencing hyperarousal.

Description

Sky Breathing is a regulation tool that harnesses the power of the breath to help children regain control and balance. It follows the 4-7-8 breathing pattern, guiding the child to breathe in blue skies and breathe out gray clouds, which can be adapted to suit the child's specific needs. It can be a soothing and effective way to settle heightened arousal and guide the child back to their window of tolerance. It's an activity you and the child can do together, like a shared adventure.

Sky Breathing

4

Breathe in blue skies.

Hold it for 7 seconds.

8

Breathe out gray skies.

Phase 8:
Re-evaluation

Client View

Remember

- **Take a playful approach:** Keep the atmosphere light and playful to ensure the child feels safe and supported. Offer the child choices to enhance their sense of safety and control during the re-evaluation process.

Description

Phase 8, re-evaluation, is a critical step in EMDR therapy for children. It involves returning to the previous target(s) to assess the child's distress levels and determine the next steps while maintaining a playful approach.

Goals

- **When returning after a previous session:** Support the client by playfully assessing the SUD rating of the previous target(s).
- **If distress is reported, return to phase 3:** If the child reports distress, go back to phase 3 to establish a fresh set of procedural steps for the target, or consider working on a related new target.

Checking Progress

Refresh the Screen

Client View

Objective

This activity is a creative tool designed to help you circle back to previous targets and assess the child's current disturbance level. It allows you to take a fresh look at old targets and evaluate any new concerns or variations.

Sample Script

For this activity, imagine that you are refreshing a computer screen to see if everything's working well. We want to know if there are any new concerns that have come up or if old ones still bother you. If there's anything new or if something from last time remains, we'll go back to phase 3 to understand them better and then continue with phases 4 through 7. You can tell me, and together we'll figure out the best way to help you.

Now let's refresh the screen together! Think about what we talked about last time, and notice how your body feels as you think about it. Rate how you are feeling using the SUD scale, with 0 being "all better" and 10 being "the worst."

Description

This activity uses the metaphor of refreshing a screen to revisit previous targets and assess the client's current level of distress. Many children can relate to this screen metaphor, making it an accessible way to understand the process.

Begin by asking the client to recall the target from the previous session and to rate their current feelings on the 10-point SUD scale. Then, gently and vaguely remind the client what you discussed last time by mentioning the previous target. This is done just enough to ignite any residual felt sense or to allow associated new material to surface, if any.

If there are new targets or remaining disturbance in old ones, return to phase 3 for assessment, then continue with phases 4 through 7. If nothing from last time remains, you can determine the appropriate next steps, whether it's more processing, resourcing, or any other clinically beneficial direction.

Refresh the Screen

When I Think of It Now

Client View

Sample Script

Let's talk about what we've worked on before and how it feels now. You can tell me using words, or if you prefer, you can write down your thoughts on this page using a dry-erase marker. It's all about helping me see if there are any remaining things that bother you and deciding what's best to focus on next.

Objective

This is a versatile tool that allows you to circle back to previous targets and assess the client's current disturbance level, either through verbal or written discussion. This provides a flexible and effective way to gauge therapeutic progress.

Description

Use the following *When I Think of It Now* template to help your client revisit what you've worked on with them up until this point. It's like having a special page where the client can talk about how things are going now. You can encourage them to discuss their experiences out loud or to even write them down if that is what they would prefer. You want to check if there is any remaining disturbance and decide what's best to work on next.

When I Think of It Now

Child's Name ______________________ Sex __________

Birthdate ______________________ Today's Date ______________________

MacArthur-Bates CDI Words and Gestures

Distributed by Paul H. Brookes Publishing Co.
1-800-638-3775; 410-337-9580
www.brookespublishing.com

Proper Mark ● Improper Marks

PART I EARLY WORDS

A. FIRST SIGNS OF UNDERSTANDING

Before children begin to speak, they show signs of understanding language by responding to familiar words and phrases. Below are some common examples. Does your child do any of these?

	Yes	No
1. Respond when name is called (e.g., by turning and looking at source).	○	○
2. Respond to "no no" (by stopping what he/she is doing, at least for a moment).	○	○
3. React to "there's mommy/daddy" by looking around for them.	○	○

B. PHRASES (28)

In the list below, please mark the phrases that your child seems to understand.

	understands		understands		understands
Are you hungry?	○	Don't touch.	○	Open your mouth.	○
Are you tired/sleepy?	○	Get up.	○	Sit down.	○
Be careful.	○	Give it to mommy.	○	Spit it out.	○
Be quiet.	○	Give me a hug.	○	Stop it.	○
Clap your hands.	○	Give me a kiss.	○	Time to go night night.	○
Change diaper.	○	Go get ____.	○	Throw the ball.	○
Come here/come on.	○	Good girl/boy.	○	This little piggy.	○
Daddy's/mommy's home.	○	Hold still.	○	Want to go for a ride?	○
Do you want more?	○	Let's go bye bye.	○		
Don't do that.	○	Look/look here.	○		

C. STARTING TO TALK

1. Some children like to "parrot" or imitate things that they've just heard (including new words that they are just learning, and/or parts of sentences, for example, repeating "work now" after mother says "Mommy's going to work now.") How often does your child imitate words? .... Never ○ Sometimes ○ Often ○

2. Some children like to go around naming or labeling things, as though proud of knowing the names and wanting to show this. How often does your child do this? .... ○ ○ ○

D. VOCABULARY CHECKLIST

The following is a list of typical words in young children's vocabularies. For words your child understands but does not yet say, place a mark in the first column (understands). For words that your child not only understands but also uses, place a mark in the second column (understands and says). If your child uses a different pronunciation of a word (for example, "raffe" for "giraffe" or "sketti" for "spaghetti"), mark the word anyway. Remember, this is a "catalogue" of words that are used by many different children. Don't worry if your child knows only a few right now.

1. SOUND EFFECTS AND ANIMAL SOUNDS (12)

	under-stands	under-stands and says		under-stands	under-stands and says		under-stands	under-stands and says
baa baa	○	○	meow	○	○	uh oh	○	○
choo choo	○	○	moo	○	○	vroom	○	○
cockadoodledoo	○	○	ouch	○	○	woof woof	○	○
grrr	○	○	quack quack	○	○	yum yum	○	○

2. ANIMALS NAMES (Real or Toy) (36)

	under-stands	under-stands and says		under-stands	under-stands and says		under-stands	under-stands and says
animal	○	○	duck	○	○	penguin	○	○
bear	○	○	elephant	○	○	pig	○	○
bee	○	○	fish	○	○	pony	○	○
bird	○	○	frog	○	○	puppy	○	○
bug	○	○	giraffe	○	○	sheep	○	○
bunny	○	○	goose	○	○	squirrel	○	○
butterfly	○	○	horse	○	○	teddy bear	○	○
cat	○	○	kitty	○	○	tiger	○	○
chicken	○	○	lamb	○	○	turkey	○	○
cow	○	○	lion	○	○	turtle	○	○
deer	○	○	monkey	○	○			
dog	○	○	mouse	○	○			
donkey	○	○	owl	○	○			

3. VEHICLES (Real or Toy) (9)

	under-stands	under-stands and says		under-stands	under-stands and says		under-stands	under-stands and says
airplane	○	○	car	○	○	stroller	○	○
bicycle	○	○	firetruck	○	○	train	○	○
bus	○	○	motorcycle	○	○	truck	○	○

4. TOYS (8)

	understands	understands and says		understands	understands and says		understands	understands and says
ball	○	○	book	○	○	pen	○	○
balloon	○	○	bubbles	○	○	toy	○	○
block	○	○	doll	○	○			

5. FOOD AND DRINK (30)

	understands	understands and says		understands	understands and says		understands	understands and says
apple	○	○	chicken	○	○	meat	○	○
banana	○	○	coffee	○	○	milk	○	○
bread	○	○	cookie	○	○	noodles	○	○
butter	○	○	cracker	○	○	orange	○	○
cake	○	○	drink	○	○	peas	○	○
candy	○	○	egg	○	○	pizza	○	○
carrots	○	○	fish	○	○	raisin	○	○
cereal	○	○	food	○	○	spaghetti	○	○
cheerios	○	○	ice cream	○	○	toast	○	○
cheese	○	○	juice	○	○	water	○	○

6. CLOTHING (19)

	understands	understands and says		understands	understands and says		understands	understands and says
beads	○	○	hat	○	○	shoe	○	○
bib	○	○	jacket	○	○	shorts	○	○
boots	○	○	jeans	○	○	sock	○	○
button	○	○	necklace	○	○	sweater	○	○
coat	○	○	pajamas	○	○	zipper	○	○
diaper	○	○	pants	○	○			
dress	○	○	shirt	○	○			

7. BODY PARTS (20)

	understands	understands and says		understands	understands and says		understands	understands and says
arm	○	○	finger	○	○	nose	○	○
belly button	○	○	hair	○	○	owie/boo boo	○	○
cheek	○	○	hand	○	○	tooth	○	○
ear	○	○	head	○	○	toe	○	○
eye	○	○	knee	○	○	tongue	○	○
face	○	○	leg	○	○	tummy	○	○
foot	○	○	mouth	○	○			

8. FURNITURE AND ROOMS (24)

	understands	understands and says		understands	understands and says		understands	understands and says
bathroom	○	○	drawer	○	○	refrigerator	○	○
bathtub	○	○	garage	○	○	rocking chair	○	○
bed	○	○	high chair	○	○	sink	○	○
bedroom	○	○	kitchen	○	○	stairs	○	○
chair	○	○	living room	○	○	stove	○	○
couch	○	○	oven	○	○	table	○	○
crib	○	○	play pen	○	○	TV	○	○
door	○	○	potty	○	○	window	○	○

9. SMALL HOUSEHOLD ITEMS (36)

	understands	understands and says		understands	understands and says		understands	understands and says
blanket	○	○	glasses	○	○	plate	○	○
bottle	○	○	hammer	○	○	purse	○	○
bowl	○	○	keys	○	○	radio	○	○
box	○	○	lamp	○	○	scissors	○	○
broom	○	○	light	○	○	soap	○	○
brush	○	○	medicine	○	○	spoon	○	○
clock	○	○	money	○	○	telephone	○	○
comb	○	○	paper	○	○	toothbrush	○	○
cup	○	○	penny	○	○	towel	○	○
dish	○	○	picture	○	○	trash	○	○
fork	○	○	pillow	○	○	vacuum	○	○
glass	○	○	plant	○	○	watch	○	○

10. OUTSIDE THINGS AND PLACES TO GO (27)

	understands	understands and says		understands	understands and says		understands	understands and says
backyard	○	○	park	○	○	snow	○	○
beach	○	○	party	○	○	star	○	○
church *	○	○	pool	○	○	store	○	○
flower	○	○	rain	○	○	sun	○	○
garden	○	○	rock	○	○	swing	○	○
home	○	○	school	○	○	tree	○	○
house	○	○	shovel	○	○	water	○	○
moon	○	○	sky	○	○	work	○	○
outside	○	○	slide	○	○	zoo	○	○

* or word used in your family

11. PEOPLE (20)

	understands	understands and says		understands	understands and says		understands	understands and says
aunt	○	○	grandma *	○	○	teacher	○	○
baby	○	○	grandpa *	○	○	uncle	○	○
babysitter	○	○	lady	○	○			
babysitter's name	○	○	man	○	○			
boy	○	○	mommy *	○	○			
brother	○	○	child's own name	○	○			
child	○	○	people	○	○			
daddy *	○	○	person	○	○			
girl	○	○	sister	○	○			

* or word used in your family

12. GAMES AND ROUTINES (19)

	understands	understands and says		understands	understands and says		understands	understands and says
bath	○	○	night night	○	○	yes	○	○
breakfast	○	○	no	○	○			
bye or bye bye	○	○	patty cake	○	○			
dinner	○	○	peekaboo	○	○			
don't	○	○	please	○	○			
hello	○	○	shh/shush/hush	○	○			
hi	○	○	thank you	○	○			
lunch	○	○	wait	○	○			
nap	○	○	wanna/want to	○	○			

13. ACTION WORDS (55)

	understands	understands and says		understands	understands and says		understands	understands and says
bite	○	○	help	○	○	show	○	○
blow	○	○	hit	○	○	sing	○	○
break	○	○	hug	○	○	sleep	○	○
bring	○	○	hurry	○	○	smile	○	○
bump	○	○	jump	○	○	splash	○	○
clean	○	○	kick	○	○	stop	○	○
close	○	○	kiss	○	○	swim	○	○
cry	○	○	look	○	○	swing	○	○
dance	○	○	love	○	○	take	○	○
draw	○	○	open	○	○	throw	○	○
drink	○	○	play	○	○	tickle	○	○
drive	○	○	pull	○	○	touch	○	○
eat	○	○	push	○	○	watch	○	○
fall	○	○	put	○	○	walk	○	○
feed	○	○	read	○	○	wash	○	○
finish	○	○	ride	○	○	wipe	○	○
get	○	○	run	○	○	write	○	○
give	○	○	say	○	○			
go	○	○	see	○	○			

14. WORDS ABOUT TIME (8)

	understands	understands and says		understands	understands and says		understands	understands and says
day	○	○	night	○	○	tomorrow	○	○
later	○	○	now	○	○	tonight	○	○
morning	○	○	today	○	○			

15. DESCRIPTIVE WORDS (37)

	understands	understands and says		understands	understands and says		understands	understands and says
all gone	○	○	empty	○	○	old	○	○
asleep	○	○	fast	○	○	pretty	○	○
bad	○	○	fine	○	○	red	○	○
big	○	○	gentle	○	○	scared	○	○
blue	○	○	good	○	○	sick	○	○
broken	○	○	happy	○	○	sleepy	○	○
careful	○	○	hard	○	○	soft	○	○
clean	○	○	hot	○	○	thirsty	○	○
cold	○	○	hungry	○	○	tired	○	○
cute	○	○	hurt	○	○	wet	○	○
dark	○	○	little	○	○	yucky	○	○
dirty	○	○	naughty	○	○			
dry	○	○	nice	○	○			

16. PRONOUNS (11)

	understands	understands and says		understands	understands and says		understands	understands and says
his	○	○	me	○	○	this	○	○
her	○	○	mine	○	○	you	○	○
I	○	○	my	○	○	your	○	○
it	○	○	that	○	○			

17. QUESTION WORDS (6)

	under-stands	under-stands and says		under-stands	under-stands and says		under-stands	under-stands and says
how	○	○	when	○	○	who	○	○
what	○	○	where	○	○	why	○	○

18. PREPOSITIONS AND LOCATIONS (11)

	under-stands	under-stands and says		under-stands	under-stands and says		under-stands	under-stands and says
away	○	○	inside	○	○	there	○	○
back	○	○	off	○	○	under	○	○
down	○	○	on	○	○	up	○	○
in	○	○	out	○	○			

19. QUANTIFIERS (8)

	under-stands	under-stands and says		under-stands	under-stands and says		under-stands	under-stands and says
all	○	○	none	○	○	same	○	○
another	○	○	not	○	○	some	○	○
more	○	○	other	○	○			

PART II ACTIONS AND GESTURES

A. FIRST COMMUNICATIVE GESTURES

When infants are first learning to communicate, they often use gestures to make their wishes known. For each item below, mark the line that describes your child's actions right now.

	Not Yet	Sometimes	Often
1. Extends arm to show you something he/she is holding.	○	○	○
2. Reaches out and gives you a toy or some object that he/she is holding.	○	○	○
3. Points (with arm and index finger extended) at some interesting object or event.	○	○	○
4. Waves bye-bye on his/her own when someone leaves.	○	○	○
5. Extends his/her arm upward to signal a wish to be picked up.	○	○	○
6. Shakes head "no".	○	○	○
7. Nods head "yes".	○	○	○
8. Gestures "hush" by placing finger to lips.	○	○	○
9. Requests something by extending arm and opening and closing hand.	○	○	○
10. Blows kisses from a distance.	○	○	○
11. Smacks lips in a "yum yum" gesture to indicate that something taste good.	○	○	○
12. Shrugs to indicate "all gone" or "where'd it go".	○	○	○

B. GAMES AND ROUTINES

Does your child do any of the following?

	Yes	No
1. Play peekaboo.	○	○
2. Play patty cake.	○	○
3. Play "so big".	○	○
4. Play chasing games.	○	○
5. Sing.	○	○
6. Dance.	○	○

C. ACTIONS WITH OBJECTS

Does your child do or try to do any of the following?

	Yes	No
1. Eat with a spoon or fork.	○	○
2. Drink from a cup containing liquid.	○	○
3. Comb or brush own hair.	○	○
4. Brush teeth.	○	○
5. Wipe face or hands with a towel or cloth.	○	○
6. Put on hat.	○	○
7. Put on a shoe or sock.	○	○
8. Put on a necklace, bracelet, or watch.	○	○
9. Lay head on hands and squeeze eyes shut as if sleeping.	○	○
10. Blow to indicate something is hot.	○	○
11. Hold plane and make it "fly".	○	○
12. Put telephone to ear.	○	○
13. Sniff flowers.	○	○
14. Push toy car or truck.	○	○
15. Throw a ball.	○	○
16. Pour pretend liquid from one container to another.	○	○
17. Stir pretend liquid in a cup or pan with a spoon.	○	○

D. PRETENDING TO BE A PARENT

Here are some things that young children sometimes do with stuffed animals or dolls. Please mark the actions that you have seen your child do.

	Yes	No
1. Put to bed.	○	○
2. Cover with blanket.	○	○
3. Feed with bottle.	○	○
4. Feed with spoon.	○	○
5. Brush/comb its hair.	○	○
6. Pat or burp it.	○	○
7. Push in stroller/buggy.	○	○
8. Rock it.	○	○
9. Kiss or hug it.	○	○
10. Try to put shoe or sock or hat on it.	○	○
11. Wipe its face or hands.	○	○
12. Talk to it.	○	○
13. Try to put diaper on it.	○	○

E. IMITATING OTHER ADULT ACTIONS (Using real or toy implements)

Does your child do or try to do any of the following?

	Yes	No
1. Sweep with broom or mop.	○	○
2. Put key in door or lock.	○	○
3. Pound with hammer or mallet.	○	○
4. Attempt to use saw.	○	○
5. "Type" at a typewriter or computer keyboard.	○	○
6. "Read" (opens book, turns page).	○	○
7. Vacuum.	○	○
8. Water plants.	○	○
9. Play musical instrument (e.g., piano, trumpet).	○	○
10. "Drive" car by turning steering wheel.	○	○
11. Wash dishes.	○	○
12. Clean with cloth or duster.	○	○
13. Write with a pen, pencil, or marker.	○	○
14. Dig with a shovel.	○	○
15. Put on glasses.	○	○

OTHER COMMENTS:

ISBN-13: 978-1-55766-888-2
ISBN-10: 1-55766-888-4